Woman's Day

Thursday Night is
Hearty Meat

The Eat-Well Cookbook of Meals in a Hurry

filipacchi
publishing

Contents

Woman'sDay

Thursday Night is
Hearty Meat

The Eat-Well Cookbook of Meals in a Hurry

❀

LAMB, PORK & VEAL • 60

CREDITS • 96

BEEF

Beef, Barley & Mushroom Soup

SLOW-COOKER • SERVES 6 • PREP: 20 MINUTES • COOK: 7 TO 9 HR ON LOW

12 oz lean beef chuck for stew

4 cups reduced-sodium chicken broth

2 cups water

1 can (14½ oz) diced tomatoes with roasted garlic and onion

12 oz shiitake mushrooms, stems removed, caps cleaned and sliced

1 large white turnip (about 7 oz), peeled and diced (1½ cups)

2 large carrots, quartered lengthwise and diced

1 cup barley (not quick-cooking)

2 large shallots, chopped (½ cup)

½ tsp each pepper and dried thyme

½ cup snipped fresh dill

SERVE WITH: sour cream

1. Mix all ingredients except dill in a 4-qt or larger slow-cooker. Cover and cook on low 7 to 9 hours until beef and vegetables are tender.

2. Stir in dill, ladle into soup bowls and top with dollops of sour cream, if desired.

PER SERVING: **264 cal, 19 g pro, 36 g car, 8 g fiber, 5 g fat (2 g sat fat), 37 mg chol, 682 mg sod**

TIP Slow-cooker heat settings can vary from brand to brand, so check for doneness after the shortest cooking time given.

Russian Beef & Vegetable Soup

ONE POT • SERVES 7 • PREP: 30 MINUTES • TOTAL TIME: 3 HR

2 tsp oil

2 Tbsp all-purpose flour

1 lb beef chuck cubes for stew, cut in ¾-in. pieces

2 cups chopped red onions

3 cans (about 14 oz each) 99%-fat-free lower-sodium beef broth

1 small bay leaf

5 cups coarsely shredded cabbage

1¼ lb small red potatoes, cut in ¾-in. cubes

8 oz carrots, peeled and thinly sliced

1 lb beets, peeled and cut in ½-in. pieces

¼ cup red wine vinegar

GARNISH: reduced-fat sour cream, chopped fresh dill

1. Heat oil in a heavy 5- to 6-qt pot over medium-high heat. Put flour and beef in a plastic bag; shake to coat beef. Add to pot and cook, stirring often, 4 minutes or until browned.

2. Stir in onions and sauté 2 to 3 minutes until they start to soften. Add beef broth and 2 cups water. Bring to a boil, scraping up any brown bits on bottom of pot. Add bay leaf. Reduce heat, cover and simmer 2 hours or until beef is tender.

3. Stir in cabbage, potatoes, carrots and beets. Cover; simmer 30 minutes or until vegetables are tender. Stir in vinegar.

4. Ladle into soup bowls. Discard bay leaf. Garnish with sour cream and dill.

PER SERVING: **319 cal, 19 g pro, 32 g car, 6 g fiber, 13 g fat (5 g sat fat), 42 mg chol, 462 mg sod**

Shepherd's Pie

ONE POT • SERVES 5 • PREP: 8 MINUTES • TOTAL TIME: 18 MINUTES

1 lb lean ground beef

1 medium onion, chopped

2 cloves garlic, minced

1 tsp dried thyme leaves

¼ tsp pepper

3 cups frozen mixed vegetables

1 can (14½ oz) diced tomatoes, drained

1 jar (12 oz) gravy (we used Heinz Bistro Au Jus)

1 container (2 lb) refrigerated mashed potatoes

2 Tbsp grated Parmesan cheese

1. Heat broiler. Heat ovenproof nonstick skillet over medium-high heat. Add ground beef, onion, garlic, thyme and pepper; cook, breaking up meat, 5 minutes or until browned. Stir in vegetables, tomatoes and gravy; simmer, covered, 5 minutes.

2. Meanwhile, heat potatoes in microwave as package directs. Drop spoonfuls of potatoes on top of beef mixture; sprinkle with Parmesan. Place under broiler for 3 to 5 minutes until topping is browned.

PER SERVING: **549 cal, 25 g pro, 46 g car, 7 g fiber, 26 g fat (12 g sat fat), 89 mg chol, 1,194 mg sod**

Chunky Beef Chili

2 lb lean beef chuck, cut for stew

1 can (28 oz) chunky-style tomatoes in purée, undrained

1½ cups chopped onions

12 oz beer or 1½ cups water

1 can (4½ oz) chopped green chiles

¼ cup tomato paste

3 Tbsp chili powder

1½ Tbsp minced garlic

2 tsp ground cumin

1½ tsp salt

¼ tsp ground cinnamon

¼ cup smooth peanut butter

3 cans (15 to 16 oz each) Roman or pinto beans, rinsed

⅓ cup chopped cilantro

SERVE WITH: sour cream, chopped red onion, shredded Cheddar cheese

1. Mix all ingredients except peanut butter, beans and cilantro in a 4-qt or larger slow-cooker.

2. Cover and cook on low 7 to 9 hours until beef is tender. Stir in peanut butter until blended, then stir in beans.

3. Cover and cook 5 minutes, or until beans are hot. Stir in cilantro.

PER SERVING: 377 cal, 32 g pro, 32 g car, 8 g fiber, 14 g fat (4 g sat fat), 74 mg chol, 1,145 mg sod

Bowl of Red

ONE POT • SERVES 6 • PREP: 10 MINUTES • TOTAL TIME: 30 MINUTES

1½ lb lean ground beef

1 large red onion, chopped

1 medium red pepper, chopped

3 Tbsp chili powder

2 tsp minced garlic

2 tsp cumin seeds or ground cumin

1 tsp dried oregano

½ tsp salt

1 can (28 oz) fire-roasted crushed tomatoes

1 can (15 oz) red kidney beans, rinsed

1 cup water

1 Tbsp chopped bittersweet chocolate (optional)

TOPPINGS: shredded Cheddar cheese, chopped red onion, red pepper and cilantro

GARNISH: sliced avocado and red pepper (optional)

1. Heat a large, deep nonstick skillet over medium-high heat. Add beef, onion and red pepper. Cook 5 minutes, stirring to break up meat, until it is no longer pink.

2. Stir in chili powder, garlic, cumin, oregano and salt. Cook, stirring, 1 minute until fragrant. Stir in tomatoes, beans and water; bring to a boil. Reduce heat, cover and simmer 15 minutes to develop flavors.

3. Remove from heat; stir in chocolate (if using) until melted. Serve with some or all of the Toppings.

PER SERVING: **411 cal, 26 g pro, 21 g car, 6 g fiber, 25 g fat (9 g sat fat), 85 mg chol, 698 mg sod**

Short Ribs

SLOW-COOKER • SERVES 4 • PREP: 10 MINUTES • COOK: 7 TO 9 HR ON LOW

1 can (about 14 oz) beef broth

1 cup chopped onion

2 small sweet potatoes, peeled, halved lengthwise and cut crosswise in ½-in.-thick slices

2 medium parsnips, peeled and diced (1½ cups)

8 oz baby carrots

4 meaty beef short ribs (about 2 lb)

¼ tsp pepper

3 sprigs fresh dill

1 can (14½ oz) diced tomatoes in juice, not drained

GARNISH: snipped dill

1. Mix all ingredients except short ribs, pepper, dill and tomatoes in a 3-qt or larger slow-cooker. Top with short ribs, sprinkle with pepper, then add dill and tomatoes.

2. Cover and cook on low 7 to 9 hours until ribs are very tender. Spoon fat off surface. Serve in shallow soup plates; sprinkle with dill.

PER SERVING: 356 cal, 23 g pro, 38 g car, 8 g fiber, 12 g fat (5 g sat), 58 mg chol, 590 mg sod

TIP The slow-cooker should be between half and three-quarters full.

Sauerbraten

SLOW-COOKER • SERVES 8 • PREP: 5 MINUTES • MARINATE: 1 TO 2 DAYS
COOK: 7 TO 9 HR ON LOW

1 cup *each* cider vinegar and water

1 Tbsp salt

6 *each* whole cloves and peppercorns

2 bay leaves

4-lb beef rump roast, visible fat trimmed

1 large onion, halved and thinly sliced

1 cup crushed gingersnaps (18 to 20 cookies)

1. In a slow-cooker liner or large bowl, combine vinegar, water, salt, cloves, peppercorns and bay leaves. Add beef and onion; seal or cover. Marinate in refrigerator 1 to 2 days, turning occasionally.

2. Remove and discard 1 cup marinade. Put liner with beef and remaining marinade in a 3½-qt or larger slow-cooker, or transfer beef and marinade from bowl to cooker.

3. Cover and cook on low 7 to 9 hours until beef is tender. Transfer beef to a cutting board; cover to keep warm. Remove and discard cloves, peppercorns and bay leaves.

4. Stir gingersnaps into liquid in cooker until dissolved. Cover and cook on high 15 minutes until thickened. Slice meat across the grain; serve with the gravy.

PER SERVING: **398 cal, 49 g pro, 17 g car, 1 g fiber, 13 g fat (4 g sat fat), 132 mg chol, 1,100 mg sod**

TIP Good with noodles, spaetzle or mashed potatoes and red cabbage.

Beef Stew Casserole

OVEN • SERVES 8 • PREP: 45 MINUTES • TOTAL TIME: 1 HR 35 MINUTES

1½ lb 1-in. cubes beef chuck (for stew)

¼ cup all-purpose flour

1½ Tbsp vegetable oil

2 cans (about 14 oz each) beef broth

1 large onion, sliced

1 Tbsp minced garlic

3 lb small sweet potatoes

1 lb *each* carrots and parsnips

3 ribs celery

1 Tbsp stick butter

¼ tsp salt

1. Position racks to divide oven in thirds. Heat to 325°F.

2. Coat beef with flour. Heat oil in a Dutch oven over medium-high heat. Add beef and brown. Add broth, onion and garlic; bring to a boil. Cover tightly and place stew on one oven rack, potatoes on other rack. Bake 30 minutes.

3. Cut carrots, parsnips and celery into 1-in. lengths; stir into stew. Cover and bake 45 minutes or until tender when pierced.

4. Peel potatoes and mash with butter and salt. Bake and serve, or cool, cover separately and refrigerate up to 3 days.

5. TO SERVE: Heat oven to 400°F. Skim fat off stew, then spoon into a shallow 3½-qt baking dish; spread potatoes over top. Bake 50 minutes or until bubbly around edges and hot in center.

PER SERVING: **488 cal, 20 g pro, 53 g car, 9 g fiber, 22 g fat (8 g sat), 66 mg chol, 550 mg sod**

Hungarian Beef Stew

SLOW-COOKER • SERVES 6 • PREP: 10 MINUTES • COOK: 8 TO 10 HR ON LOW

1¼ lb lean beef chuck for stew, cut in ¾-in. pieces

1 lb carrots, sliced

2 medium onions, thinly sliced

3 cups thinly sliced cabbage

2 cups water, or ½ cup red wine plus 1½ cups water

1 can (6 oz) tomato paste

1 envelope onion-mushroom soup mix (from a 1.8-oz box)

1 Tbsp paprika

1 tsp caraway seeds

1 cup (8 oz) reduced-fat sour cream

SERVE WITH: egg noodles

1. Mix all ingredients except sour cream in a 3½-qt or larger slow-cooker.

2. Cover and cook on low 8 to 10 hours until tender. Turn off cooker and stir in sour cream until well blended.

PER SERVING: **308 cal, 24 g pro, 25 g car, 6 g fiber, 13 g fat (5 g sat fat), 74 mg chol, 624 mg sod**

Glazed Corned Beef

1 thin-cut corned beef brisket (about 2¾ lb), fat trimmed

¼ cup apple jelly

¼ cup sweet-hot or honey mustard

1. Heat oven to 350°F. Put corned beef in a Dutch oven, add water to cover and bring to a boil.

2. Cover and bake 3½ to 4 hours until fork-tender. Remove from oven.

3. Heat broiler. Line a rimmed baking sheet with nonstick foil. Place beef on sheet.

4. Whisk jelly and mustard in a bowl until smooth. Spoon about ½ the glaze over beef.

5. Broil 2 minutes or until glaze bubbles. Remove to a cutting board; thinly slice across the grain. Serve with remaining glaze.

PER SERVING: **275 cal, 24 g pro, 14 g car, 0 g fiber, 14 g fat (4 g sat fat), 89 mg chol, 2,674 mg sod**

DIFFERENT TAKES

Instead of cooking corned beef in oven, simmer in slow-cooker 10 to 11 hours on low. Glaze and broil as directed.

Add some pickling spices to the cooking water.

Make Reuben wraps with leftovers: Spread wraps with Russian dressing; top with sliced corned beef, Swiss cheese and sauerkraut; roll up.

Cuban Ropa Vieja

SLOW-COOKER • SERVES 4 • PREP: 15 MINUTES • COOK: 8 TO 10 HR ON LOW

2 cubanelle or Italian frying peppers, seeded and sliced

1 cup sliced onion

1 can (8 oz) tomato sauce

¼ cup tomato paste

1 Tbsp *each* olive oil, cider vinegar and minced garlic

1 tsp ground cumin

1 bay leaf

½ tsp salt

1½-lb boneless chuck steak

⅓ cup coarsely chopped alcaparrado (we used Goya), or ⅓ cup pimiento-stuffed olives plus 2 Tbsp chopped capers

⅓ cup chopped cilantro

1. Mix all ingredients except steak, alcaparrado and cilantro in a 3½-qt or larger slow-cooker. Top with steak; turn steak over to coat with mixture.

2. Cover and cook on low 8 to 10 hours until steak is very tender. Transfer steak to a cutting board. Remove and discard bay leaf. Tear steak in shreds using two forks. Return shreds to cooker; stir in alcaparrado and chopped cilantro, and serve.

PER SERVING: **541 cal, 32 g pro, 15 g car, 3 g fiber, 40 g fat (14 g sat fat), 123 mg chol, 1,098 mg sod**

Rio Grande Pot Roast

SLOW-COOKER • SERVES 8 • PREP: 5 MINUTES • COOK: 8 TO 10 HR ON LOW

1½ cups thick-and-chunky salsa

1 cup beer or water

1 can (6 oz) tomato paste

1 pkt (1.25 oz) taco seasoning

3-lb boneless beef bottom round roast

½ tsp *each* salt and pepper

2 tbsp peanut butter

⅓ cup chopped cilantro

1. Mix first 4 ingredients in a 5-qt or larger slow-cooker. Rub beef with salt and pepper; add to cooker. Spoon some sauce mixture over top.

2. Cover and cook on low 8 to 10 hours until beef is very tender. Remove to a cutting board. Stir peanut butter and cilantro into sauce. Slice meat against the grain; serve with the sauce.

PER SERVING: 432 cal, 36 g pro,
11 g car, 1 g fiber, 25 g fat (9 g sat fat),
109 mg chol, 1,112 mg sod

Stuffed Cabbage with Cranberry & Tomato Sauce

SLOW-COOKER • SERVES 6 • PREP: 35 MINUTES • COOK: ABOUT 7½ HR ON LOW

1½ lb lean ground beef

⅓ cup uncooked parboiled (converted) rice

1 large egg

¾ tsp ground allspice

1 tsp salt

½ tsp pepper

12 savoy cabbage leaves (see Note)

1 can (16 oz) whole-berry cranberry sauce

1 can (14½ oz) diced tomatoes with onion and garlic

½ cup raisins, preferably golden

⅓ cup packed light-brown sugar

¼ cup fresh lemon juice

1. You'll need a 5-qt or larger slow-cooker.

2. Mix first 6 ingredients in a bowl. Spoon a slightly rounded ¼ cup of mixture on bottom center of each cabbage leaf; turn in sides and roll up.

3. Stack in cooker, seam sides down. Top with remaining ingredients. Cover and cook on low 7 hours or until cabbage is soft and meat mixture is cooked through.

PER SERVING: **584 cal, 24 g pro, 67 g car, 2 g fiber, 24 g fat (10 g sat fat), 121 mg chol, 821 mg sod**

NOTE The crinkled leaves of savoy cabbage are quite soft and pliable, so precooking is unnecessary. Cut the hard rib from each leaf. If savoy cabbage is unavailable, freeze a head of regular green cabbage at least 24 hours. As the head thaws, the leaves should become soft and peel off easily.

Italian Meatballs with Marinara Sauce

OVEN & SLOW-COOKER • SERVES 6 • PREP: 50 MINUTES • COOK: 6 TO 7 HR ON LOW

12 oz ground beef

12 oz ground pork

¼ cup chopped onion

2 cloves garlic, finely chopped

2 tsp Italian seasoning

¼ cup Italian-style dried bread crumbs

1 large egg, lightly beaten

1 jar (28 oz) marinara sauce

1. Heat oven to 375°F. Line a 15 x 10 x 1-in. baking pan with aluminum foil; coat with nonstick cooking spray.

2. Mix all ingredients except the marinara sauce in a bowl until well combined. Shape mixture into 24 balls about 1½ in. in diameter (see Tip). Place in baking pan.

3. Bake 30 to 35 minutes, until meat is no longer pink in the center. Place meatballs in a 3½- to 4-qt slow-cooker. Pour marinara sauce over meatballs.

4. Cover and cook on low 6 to 7 hours to blend flavors.

5. Serve with pasta (see Tip).

PER SERVING: 329 cal, 28 g pro, 16 g car, 3 g fiber, 17 g fat (6 g sat fat), 103 mg chol, 693 mg sod

TIPS To make perfectly round meatballs, use a small ice cream scoop. If you use your hands, be sure not to over-handle the meat, or it will become too tightly packed to let the sauce sink in.

Instead of pasta, try meatballs on a bed of polenta. If you prefer the classic spaghetti approach, though, give thicker, chewier pastas like perciatelli or bucatini a try.

Mexican Rolled Flank Steak

SLOW-COOKER • SERVES 5 • PREP: 25 MINUTES • COOK: 8 TO 10 HR ON LOW

1 flank steak (1½ lb)
1 box (6 oz) cornbread stuffing mix
1 cup thick-and-chunky salsa
¼ cup chopped fresh cilantro

1. Ask your butcher to butterfly the flank steak, or you can do it yourself: Lay meat on a cutting board with the grain running vertically. Using a long, sharp knife, cut the meat almost in half, opening it like a book but stopping before going all the way through. Cut several 12-in. pieces of kitchen twine and space evenly under steak.

2. Toss cornbread stuffing with 1 cup boiling water and ½ cup salsa until moistened; stir in cilantro. Spread over steak, leaving about 1 inch along edges. Roll steak starting from a long side, jelly-roll style; tie with twine.

3. Place seam side down in a 6-qt oval slow-cooker. Spoon remaining ½ cup salsa over meat. Cover and cook on low 8 to 10 hours.

4. Remove steak to a cutting board; let rest 10 minutes. Discard cooking liquid. Remove string and cut steak into ½-in.-thick slices. Serve with additional salsa, if desired.

PER SERVING: **370 cal, 33 g pro, 28 g car, 2 g fiber, 12 g fat (5 g sat fat), 57 mg chol, 936 mg sod**

Beef Negamaki

GRILL • SERVES 4 • PREP: 15 MINUTES • MARINATE: 30 TO 60 MINUTES
COOK: 5 MINUTES

12 scallions, ends trimmed

4 thin-cut top round steaks
(1 to 1¼ lb total)

¾ cup classic stir-fry sauce

3 Tbsp *each* sugar and water

1. Microwave scallions in a loosely covered pie plate on high 1 minute to soften.

2. Place each steak between sheets of plastic wrap. Gently pound until about 8 x 6 in. and ⅛ in. thick. Lay 3 scallions down length of each piece; tightly roll up from a long side. Secure with wooden toothpicks. Put in a large ziptop bag.

3. In a microwave-safe bowl, stir sauce, sugar and water until sugar dissolves. Add ⅓ cup of mixture to bag; refrigerate 30 to 60 minutes.

4. Heat outdoor grill or stovetop grill pan. Grill negamaki 5 minutes, turning to brown on all sides. Discard marinade.

5. Remove toothpicks; trim ends of negamaki, then cut alternately straight across and diagonally in 2-in. lengths.

6. Microwave sauce in bowl to heat; serve with negamaki.

PER SERVING: **313 cal, 29 g pro, 27 g car, 1 g fiber, 13 g fat (5 g sat fat), 75 mg chol, 920 mg sod**

DIFFERENT TAKES

Substitute thin asparagus spears for the scallions.

Stir some wasabi into the stir-fry sauce mixture.

Sprinkle negamaki with toasted sesame seeds before serving.

Meatball Stew

SLOW-COOKER • SERVES 4 • PREP: 14 MINUTES • COOK: 7 TO 9 HR ON LOW

1 can (10¾ oz) condensed cream of mushroom soup with roasted garlic

½ cup beef broth

4 large red potatoes, cut in 1-in. chunks

1½ cups baby carrots

MEATBALLS

1 lb lean ground beef

½ cup grated Parmesan cheese

⅓ cup seasoned dried bread crumbs

1 large egg

2 Tbsp chopped fresh parsley

½ tsp *each* salt and pepper

GARNISH: chopped parsley

1. Stir soup and broth in a 3-qt or larger slow-cooker until blended. Stir in potatoes and carrots.

2. Mix Meatball ingredients in a bowl with your hands or a wooden spoon until blended. Form into 1½-in. balls. Place on top of vegetable mixture.

3. Cover and cook on low 7 to 9 hours until meatballs are cooked through and vegetables are tender.

4. Transfer meatballs and vegetables to a platter with a slotted spoon. Whisk sauce until smooth, and pour over meatballs and vegetables. Sprinkle servings with parsley.

PER SERVING: **661 cal, 33 g pro, 62 g car, 5 g fiber, 30 g fat (12 g sat fat), 148 mg chol, 1,483 mg sod**

Spicy Glazed Meat Loaf

SLOW-COOKER • SERVES 6 • PREP: 10 MINUTES
COOK: 4 HR ON HIGH, 8 TO 10 HR ON LOW

¾ cup spicy or regular ketchup

1½ lbs lean ground beef

¾ cup seasoned bread crumbs

½ cup finely chopped onion

¼ cup grated Parmesan cheese

1 large egg

1½ Tbsp Worcestershire sauce

2 tsp minced garlic

1 tsp salt

½ tsp ground pepper

1. To ease removal of the meat loaf from the cooker, fold two 24-in.-long pieces of aluminum foil in half lengthwise, then in half lengthwise again. Place strips across each other, forming a "+" in bottom of a 3-qt or larger slow-cooker. Press strips against inside of cooker, letting ends hang over the outside.

2. In a large bowl, mix ½ cup ketchup with the remaining ingredients until well blended. Form into a 7 x 4 x 2-in. loaf. Place in cooker; spread top and sides of loaf with remaining ¼ cup ketchup.

3. Cover and cook on high 4 hours or on low 8 to 10 hours, until a meat thermometer inserted in center of meat loaf registers 160°F.

PER SERVING: 425 cal, 25 g pro, 21 g car, 1 g fiber, 26 g fat (10 g sat fat), 123 mg chol, 1,356 mg sod

Chicken Minestrone with Pesto

SLOW-COOKER • SERVES 6 • PREP: 15 MINUTES • COOK: 7 TO 9 HR ON LOW
FINISH: 15 MINUTES ON HIGH

1 can (28 oz) diced tomatoes in juice, undrained

4 cups chicken broth

1 lb boneless, skinless chicken thighs, cut in 1-in. chunks

1 medium baking potato, peeled and diced

½ cup *each* chopped onion, carrot and celery

¼ tsp pepper

1 can (16 oz) white kidney beans (cannellini), rinsed

1 medium zucchini, diced

1 cup frozen cut green beans, thawed

⅓ cup refrigerated prepared basil pesto

1. Mix all ingredients except the cannellini beans, zucchini, green beans and pesto in a 4-qt or larger slow-cooker.

2. Cover and cook on low 7 to 9 hours until chicken is cooked through and vegetables are tender.

3. Stir in cannellini beans, zucchini and green beans. Cover and cook on high 15 minutes, or until zucchini is tender.

4. Spoon into bowls; top servings with pesto.

PER SERVING: 289 cal, 25 g pro, 27 g car, 6 g fiber, 9 g fat (2 g sat fat), 67 mg chol, 827 mg sod

Grilled Chicken Risotto

SKILLET & GRILL • SERVES 4 • PREP: 10 MINUTES • TOTAL TIME: 30 MINUTES

1 box (5.5 oz) Creamy Parmesan Risotto

2 medium zucchini, sliced lengthwise ½ in. thick

2 boneless, skinless chicken breasts (about 12 oz)

1 Tbsp oil

½ tsp pepper

¼ cup frozen peas, thawed

1 medium tomato, diced

1. Cook risotto as package directs.

2. Meanwhile, heat stovetop grill pan. Brush zucchini and chicken with oil, then sprinkle with pepper.

3. Grill zucchini 7 to 9 minutes and chicken 10 to 12 minutes, turning once, until zucchini is tender and chicken is cooked through.

4. Remove chicken and zucchini to cutting board; cut into bite-size pieces.

5. When risotto is finished cooking, stir in peas, tomato, chicken and zucchini; remove from heat.

PER SERVING: **295 cal, 24 g pro, 33 g car, 3 g fiber, 8 g fat (2 g sat fat), 50 mg chol, 546 mg sod**

Mexican Chicken Potpie

OVEN • SERVES 4 • PREP: 10 MINUTES • TOTAL TIME: 55 MINUTES

2 burrito-size flour tortillas, warmed

1 can (10¾ oz) 25%-less-sodium condensed cream of mushroom soup

2 cups shredded cooked chicken

1 bag (16 oz) frozen mixed vegetables, thawed

1 can (4½ oz) chopped green chiles

⅓ cup chopped cilantro

½ tsp minced garlic

Nonstick spray

1. Heat oven to 375°F. Line a 9-in. pie plate with a warmed tortilla.

2. Mix soup, chicken, vegetables, chiles, cilantro and garlic. Spoon into lined pie plate. Top with remaining tortilla and tuck in edges. Coat with nonstick spray.

3. Cover with foil and bake 20 minutes. Uncover and bake 25 more minutes, or until top is golden and filling is hot.

PER SERVING: 380 cal, 26 g pro, 40 g car, 8 g fiber, 13 g fat (3 g sat fat), 56 mg chol, 858 mg sod

Italian Sausage Lasagna

OVEN • SERVES 8 • PREP: 30 MINUTES • TOTAL TIME: ABOUT 1¾ HR

1 lb Italian turkey sausage, removed from casing

15 oz part-skim ricotta

1 cup parsley, chopped

¾ cup grated Parmesan cheese

1½ cup marinara sauce

9 oven-ready lasagna noodles

1 jar (16 oz) Alfredo sauce

½ cup sun-dried tomato pesto (from a 10-oz jar)

2 cups shredded mozzarella cheese

1. Heat oven to 375°F. You'll need a 13 x 9-in. baking dish coated with nonstick spray.

2. Sauté sausage, breaking up chunks, until no longer pink.

3. Mix ricotta, parsley and Parmesan in a bowl until blended.

4. Spread ¾ cup marinara sauce in prepared baking dish. Place 3 noodles crosswise on sauce. Spread ¾ cup Alfredo sauce on noodles, then sprinkle on ½ the sausage. Top with dollops of ½ the ricotta mixture and ½ the pesto; spread evenly. Top with ⅓ the mozzarella. Repeat layers once, starting with noodles (omitting marinara). Top with remaining noodles, marinara and Alfredo sauces, and mozzarella.

5. Cover baking dish with foil; bake 1 hour or until bubbly at edges. Uncover; bake 5 minutes more to brown top.

PER SERVING: **573 cal, 31 g pro, 35 g car, 3 g fiber, 35 g fat (15 g sat fat), 123 mg chol, 1,429 mg sod**

Sausage & Pepper Pies

OVEN • SERVES 4 • PREP: 15 MINUTES • TOTAL TIME: 28 MINUTES

2 tsp olive oil

½ lb turkey sausage, casing removed

2 cubanelle peppers, seeded and sliced

1 red bell pepper, seeded and sliced

1 medium red onion, sliced

2 cloves garlic, chopped

1 tube (13.8 oz) refrigerated pizza crust

1 cup shredded Italian blend cheese

Marinara sauce (optional)

1. Heat oven to 425°F. Coat 2 large baking sheets with nonstick cooking spray.

2. Heat oil in a skillet. Add sausage and cook, breaking up, 3 minutes. Add peppers and onion, and cook 6 minutes or until sausage is cooked and vegetables are softened. Stir in garlic; cook 30 seconds.

3. Unroll dough onto a floured surface. Cut into 4 pieces; shape each into a 6½-in. square. Place on baking sheets. Divide sausage mixture and cheese among the pieces. Bring one corner of dough to opposite corner; seal.

4. Bake 15 to 18 minutes until golden. Serve marinara sauce on the side, if desired.

PER SERVING: **478 cal, 25 g pro, 56 g car, 3 g fiber, 18 g fat (7 g sat fat), 54 mg chol, 1,313 mg sod**

Roasted Chicken & Root Vegetables

OVEN • SERVES 6 • PREP: 20 MINUTES • TOTAL TIME: 1½ HR

1 roasting chicken (5½ lb), giblets reserved for another use

½ tsp each salt, pepper and dried thyme

6 small red potatoes, halved

½ small rutabaga, peeled and cut in 1½-in. chunks

1 medium red onion, cut in 12 wedges

2 large carrots, cut in 2-in. lengths, thicker parts halved lengthwise

3 small parsnips, peeled and cut in 2-in. lengths, thicker parts halved lengthwise

1. Heat oven to 400°F. You'll need a large roasting pan lined with nonstick foil. Place chicken on foil and sprinkle with half the salt, pepper and thyme.

2. Roast chicken 25 minutes. Add vegetables to pan (if there's not enough room in pan, place on a nonstick foil–lined rimmed baking sheet). Sprinkle with remaining salt, pepper and thyme, and toss to coat with drippings.

3. Roast 35 to 45 minutes longer, tossing vegetables once or twice, until vegetables are tender and a meat thermometer inserted in the thickest part of the thigh, not touching bone, registers 170°F.

4. Remove chicken to cutting board; let rest 5 minutes before carving. Arrange on platter with vegetables.

PER SERVING: **642 cal, 51 g pro, 38 g car, 5 g fiber, 31 g fat (9 g sat fat), 152 mg chol, 377 mg sod**

Chicken Parmesan

OVEN • SERVES 5 • PREP: 10 MINUTES • TOTAL TIME: 30 MINUTES

½ cup dried bread crumbs

¼ cup grated Parmesan cheese

½ tsp garlic powder

¼ tsp salt

1 to 2 Tbsp olive oil

1¼ lb thin-sliced skinless, boneless chicken breast cutlets

1 cup pasta sauce

1 cup shredded part-skim mozzarella cheese

SERVE WITH: whole-wheat spaghetti and a salad

1. Heat oven to 425°F. Coat a rimmed baking sheet with nonstick spray.

2. Combine bread crumbs, Parmesan, garlic powder and salt in a shallow dish. Place olive oil in another shallow dish. Lightly coat each cutlet with oil, then coat evenly with bread-crumb mixture. Arrange chicken on baking sheet.

3. Bake 12 to 14 minutes until chicken is cooked through. Leave oven on.

4. Spoon sauce evenly over chicken and sprinkle with mozzarella.

5. Bake 5 minutes or until cheese melts.

PER SERVING: 450 cal, 44 g pro, 16 g car, 1 g fiber, 23 g fat (8 g sat fat), 152 mg chol, 610 mg sod

Mini Meat Loaves

OVEN • SERVES 6 • PREP: 15 MINUTES • TOTAL TIME: 35 MINUTES

3 slices whole-grain bread

1 lb ground turkey

½ lb lean ground beef

Whites from 2 large eggs

2 Tbsp minced dried onion flakes

2 tsp Worcestershire sauce

¼ tsp *each* garlic powder and salt

1 pkg (10 oz) frozen chopped spinach, thawed and drained

6 Tbsp ketchup

1. Heat oven to 425°F. You'll need a rimmed baking sheet lined with nonstick foil.

2. Tear bread into food processor. Pulse to make coarse crumbs. Add remaining ingredients and 2 Tbsp of the ketchup. Pulse just until blended. Form into 6 loaves (5 x 2½ in. each, about 1 scant cup per loaf) on lined pan.

3. Evenly spread tops with remaining 4 Tbsp ketchup. Bake 20 minutes until cooked through and instant-read thermometer inserted in center registers 160°F.

PER SERVING: **257 cal, 27 g pro, 13 g car, 2 g fiber, 11 g fat (3 g sat fat), 78 mg chol, 473 mg sod**

Chicken & Kielbasa Gumbo

ONE POT • SERVES 4 • PREP: 5 MINUTES • TOTAL TIME: 20 MINUTES

7 oz lowfat kielbasa (½ a 14-oz pkg), sliced ¼ in. thick

2½ cups chicken broth

1 can (14½ oz) Cajun stewed tomatoes

1½ cups frozen pepper stir-fry mixture (yellow, green and red bell pepper strips and onions)

1 box (10 oz) frozen sliced okra, thawed

1 cup uncooked 5-minute rice

1 box (10 oz) refrigerated skinless, fully cooked chicken breast, shredded, or 2 cups shredded cooked chicken

1. Cook kielbasa in a 3-qt saucepan over medium-high heat, stirring often, 3 minutes or until lightly browned.

2. Add broth, tomatoes and stir-fry mixture. Cover and bring to a boil over high heat. Add okra; simmer 3 minutes. Stir in rice.

3. Cover and simmer 1 to 2 minutes, or until vegetables and rice are tender. Stir in chicken; heat and serve.

PER SERVING: **319 cal, 31 g pro, 36 g car, 3 g fiber, 6 g fat (3 g sat fat), 70 mg chol, 1,522 mg sod**

Chicken Pumpkin Stew

1 Tbsp canola oil

1½ lb skinless, boneless chicken thighs, visible fat trimmed, cut in 1-in. pieces

1 medium onion, chopped

1 red pepper, cut in 1-in. pieces

1 tsp minced garlic

1 can (14½ oz) *each* chicken broth and diced tomatoes

1 Tbsp smoked paprika

½ tsp salt

3 cups 1-in. cubes peeled sugar pumpkin or butternut squash (1 lb)

8 oz fresh green beans, cut in half

1 Tbsp cornstarch

¼ cup reduced-fat creamy peanut butter

1. Heat oil in large saucepan over medium-high heat. Add chicken; sauté 4 minutes or until browned. Remove to a plate. Reduce heat to medium. Add onion, pepper and garlic; sauté 4 minutes or until softened.

2. Add 1½ cups broth, the tomatoes, paprika and salt. Bring to a boil; add chicken, pumpkin and beans. Reduce heat, cover and simmer 12 minutes or until chicken and pumpkin are tender.

3. Meanwhile stir remaining broth, the cornstarch and peanut butter in a bowl until smooth. Add to pot; stir until blended. Cook 2 minutes or until thickened.

PER SERVING: **291 cal, 28 g pro, 21 g car, 2 g fiber, 11 g fat(2 g sat fat), 94 mg chol, 616 mg sod**

Green Turkey Chili

1 medium onion, chopped

2 turkey thighs (1 lb each), skin removed

1 can (15½ oz) white kidney beans (cannellini), rinsed

1 can (11 oz) corn, drained

1½ cups medium green tomatilla salsa

1 can (4.5 oz) chopped green chiles

2 tsp minced garlic

1½ tsp ground cumin

½ tsp salt

⅓ cup chopped cilantro

SERVE WITH: sour cream, shredded Monterey Jack cheese, chopped red onion and lime wedges

1. Put turkey thighs on top of onion in a 3½-qt or larger slow-cooker. Add beans and corn. Mix salsa, chiles, garlic, cumin and salt in a medium bowl; pour over top.

2. Cover and cook on low 8 to 10 hours until meat is tender. Remove turkey to a cutting board. Cut bite-size; discard bones.

3. Return meat to cooker; stir in cilantro.

PER SERVING: **323 cal, 34 g pro, 34 g car, 7 g fiber, 7 g fat (2 g sat fat), 97 mg chol, 1,373 mg sod**

Apple-Chicken Curry

SLOW-COOKER • SERVES 8 • PREP: 15 MINUTES • COOK: 4 HR ON LOW

2½ lb boneless, skinless chicken thighs and/or breasts

¾ tsp salt

½ tsp freshly ground black pepper

2 apples, peeled if desired, cored and cut in ½-in.-thick slices

3 cups green and/or red bell pepper, seeded and cut in chunks

1 can (about 14 oz) diced tomatoes in juice, undrained

1 cup apple juice

1 Tbsp curry powder

2 tsp chopped garlic

½ cup raisins

Cooked rice (optional)

1. Sprinkle chicken pieces with salt and pepper; place in a slow-cooker along with apples.

2. In a large skillet, combine bell peppers, tomatoes with their juice, apple juice, curry powder and garlic; bring to a boil. Stir in raisins. Pour over chicken and apples in slow-cooker.

3. Cover and cook on low 4 hours, or until chicken is cooked through. Serve over cooked rice, if desired.

PER SERVING: 251 cal, 32 g pro, 22 g car, 3 g fiber, 4 g fat (1 g sat fat), 100 mg chol, 524 mg sod

Moroccan Chicken & Couscous

ONE POT • SERVES 5 • PREP: 5 MINUTES • TOTAL TIME: 30 MINUTES

2 tsp olive oil

4 boneless, skinless chicken thighs, each cut into 3 pieces

¼ tsp salt

1 can (14½ oz) chicken broth

1 can (14½ oz) diced tomatoes with garlic and onion

1 pkg (about 1 lb) cubed fresh butternut squash

½ cup raisins

2 tsp ground cumin

1 tsp *each* ground cinnamon and smoked paprika

1 cup plain couscous

1 cup frozen peas

1. Heat oil in large deep skillet over medium-high heat. Sprinkle chicken with salt and cook 5 minutes, turning once, until browned. Add broth, tomatoes, squash, raisins, cumin, cinnamon and paprika. Bring to a boil; cover and reduce heat. Simmer 15 minutes or until chicken is tender.

2. Stir in couscous and peas, and bring to a boil. Cover, remove skillet from heat and let stand 5 minutes.

PER SERVING: **347 cal, 20 g pro, 58 g car, 7 g fiber, 5 g fat (1 g sat fat), 45 mg chol, 752 mg sod**

Skillet Chicken & Chickpeas

SKILLET • SERVES 4 • PREP: 15 MINUTES • COOK: 30 MINUTES

2 tsp oil

1 medium onion, sliced

2 cloves garlic, minced

1½ tsp ground cumin

½ tsp *each* ground cinnamon, ginger and salt

¼ tsp pepper

1 can (28 oz) diced tomatoes

4 *each* chicken drumsticks and thighs, skinned (2¼ lb)

1 can (15 oz) chickpeas, rinsed

1 small butternut squash, peeled, seeded and cubed (3 cups)

⅓ cup raisins

GARNISH: chopped cilantro, toasted almonds (optional)

1. Heat oil in a large nonstick skillet over medium-high heat. Sauté onion 2 minutes. Add garlic and spices; cook 30 seconds until fragrant.

2. Stir in tomatoes and their juices until blended. Add chicken and chickpeas. Bring to a boil; cover, reduce heat and simmer 15 minutes.

3. Add butternut squash and raisins; simmer, covered, 10 to 15 minutes more until squash is tender and chicken is cooked through. If desired, garnish with cilantro and almonds; serve with couscous.

PER SERVING: **460 cal, 38 g pro, 58 g car, 12 g fiber, 9 g fat (2 g sat fat), 116 mg chol, 889 mg sod**

Picadillo Stuffed Peppers

SLOW-COOKER • SERVES 4 • PREP: 15 MINUTES • COOK: 5 TO 6 HR ON LOW

1 jar (26 oz) marinara sauce

1 Tbsp red-wine vinegar

½ tsp ground cumin

¼ tsp ground cinnamon

4 large peppers

8 oz ground chicken

1 small zucchini, diced

½ cup quick-cooking barley

⅓ cup finely chopped onion

¼ cup raisins

1. Stir marinara sauce, vinegar, cumin and cinnamon in large bowl until mixed well. Spoon 1½ cups sauce into bottom of 5-qt or larger slow-cooker. Slice off top ½ in. of peppers; seed them and reserve tops.

2. Add ground chicken, zucchini, barley, onion and raisins to remaining sauce in bowl; mix well. Evenly spoon mixture into peppers and replace tops. Stand peppers upright in slow-cooker.

3. Cover and cook on low 5 to 6 hours, until peppers are tender and instant-read thermometer inserted in filling registers 160°F. Serve with sauce.

PER SERVING: 330 cal, 16 g pro, 52 g car, 9 g fiber, 8 g fat (2 g sat fat), 39 mg chol, 783 mg sod

Cranberry-Chipotle Turkey

SLOW-COOKER • SERVES 4 • PREP: 10 MINUTES • COOK: 8 TO 10 HR ON LOW

1 large onion, thinly sliced

2 turkey thighs (about 2 lb), skin and excess fat removed

1 can (16 oz) whole cranberry sauce

½ cup salt-free Southwestern chipotle marinade

1. Place onion, then turkey thighs in a 3½-qt or larger slow-cooker.

2. Stir ½ cup cranberry sauce and ¼ cup chipotle marinade in small bowl until blended. Spoon over thighs to coat.

3. Cover and cook on low 8 to 10 hours until turkey is tender. Remove turkey thighs to cutting board. Cut meat in large pieces from both sides of each thigh bone and slice.

4. Remove onion from cooking liquid with slotted spoon; discard cooking liquid. Microwave remaining cranberry sauce and chipotle marinade about 2 minutes until melted. Stir in onion and spoon over turkey.

PER SERVING: 415 cal, 37 g pro, 41 g car, 2 g fiber, 11 g fat (3 g sat fat), 108 mg chol, 145 mg sod

Moroccan Lamb Shanks

SLOW-COOKER • SERVES 4 • PREP: 20 MINUTES • COOK: 10 TO 12 HR ON LOW

2 cans (15½ oz each) chickpeas, rinsed

1 cup *each* pitted prunes and dried apricot halves

1 cup finely chopped onion

1 Tbsp minced garlic

1 cup chicken broth

¼ cup fresh orange juice

1 Tbsp freshly grated orange zest

½ tsp *each* salt, ground cinnamon, cumin and ginger

4 lamb shanks (12 to 14 oz each)

GARNISH: toasted sliced almonds and chopped parsley

1. Mix all ingredients except lamb in an oval 5½-qt or larger slow-cooker. Add lamb; spoon some mixture over shanks.

2. Cover and cook on low 10 to 12 hours until lamb is very tender.

3. Remove lamb to serving plates; spoon out chickpeas and fruit with a slotted spoon and add to plates. Pour liquid into a bowl, skim off fat and pour juices into a gravy boat. Serve with the lamb; garnish plates with almonds and parsley.

PER SERVING: 850 cal, 69 g pro, 74 g car, 12 g fiber, 31 g fat (11 g sat fat), 196 mg chol, 931 mg sod

Curried Lamb

4 cups 1-in. chunks peeled butternut squash (about half of a 2½-lb squash)

1½ lb lamb stew meat

1 jar (15 oz) tikka masala cooking sauce

1 cup frozen peas

1. Stir butternut squash, lamb and ¾ cup cooking sauce in a 3½-qt or larger slow-cooker.

2. Cover and cook on low 8 to 10 hours until lamb and butternut squash are tender. Stir in peas and remaining cooking sauce 15 minutes before end of cooking.

PER SERVING: **398 cal, 23 g pro, 18 g car, 3 g fiber, 26 g fat (10 g sat fat), 79 mg chol, 553 mg sod**

Lamb Stew with Dried Fruit

SLOW-COOKER • SERVES 6 • PREP: 15 MINUTES • COOK: 7 TO 9 HR ON LOW

3 cups chopped onions

2¼-lb lamb shoulder,
cut in 1½-in. chunks

2 sweet potatoes, peeled and
cut in 1½-in. chunks

2 cinnamon sticks (each about
3 in. long)

1 cup *each* dried apricots and
pitted prunes

1 Tbsp *each* minced garlic and
fresh ginger

½ tsp salt

¼ tsp ground red pepper (cayenne)

1 can (14 oz) chicken broth

1 box (10 oz) couscous

⅓ cup slivered almonds, toasted

1. Layer onions, lamb, sweet potatoes, cinnamon sticks, apricots and prunes in a 4½-qt or larger slow-cooker. Top with garlic, ginger, salt and pepper; add broth.

2. Cover and cook on low 7 to 9 hours until lamb and potatoes are tender.

3. Remove solids with a slotted spoon to a serving bowl. Pour liquid into a bowl, skim off fat and add juices to stew.

4. Prepare couscous as package directs. Serve with the stew, and sprinkle stew with the almonds.

PER SERVING: 742 cal, 46 g pro,
104 g car, 10 g fiber, 16 g fat (5 g sat
fat), 112 mg chol, 471 mg sod

Greek Lamb & Spinach Stew

SLOW-COOKER • SERVES 6 • PREP: 10 MINUTES • COOK: 7 TO 9 HR ON LOW

2-lb boneless lamb shoulder, visible fat trimmed, cut in 1-in. pieces

1 can (14½ oz) diced tomatoes

½ cup chopped onion

1 Tbsp minced garlic

½ tsp *each* Greek herb seasoning and salt

¼ tsp pepper

1 can (19 oz) cannellini beans, rinsed

1 can (13.75 oz) whole artichoke hearts, cut in half

3 cups baby spinach (3 oz)

2 tsp grated lemon zest

GARNISH: crumbled feta cheese

1. Mix lamb pieces, tomatoes, onion, garlic, Greek seasoning, salt and pepper in a 3½-qt or larger slow-cooker.

2. Cover and cook on low 7 to 9 hours until lamb is tender when pierced.

3. Mash 1 cup beans. Stir mashed and whole beans, artichoke hearts and spinach into cooker.

4. Cover and cook on high 15 minutes or until spinach wilts and mixture is hot.

5. Stir in lemon zest; sprinkle with feta.

PER SERVING: **325 cal, 36 g pro, 19 g car, 6 g fiber, 11 g fat (4 g sat fat), 100 mg chol, 619 mg sod**

TIP Good served with orzo.

65

Sweet-Spicy Lamb Tagine

SLOW-COOKER • SERVES 6 • PREP: 35 MINUTES
COOK: 4 TO 5 HR ON HIGH, 8 TO 10 HR ON LOW

1 tsp *each* ground cumin, cinnamon, ginger and coriander

2 Tbsp olive oil

1 boneless leg of lamb (4 to 6 lb), trimmed of fat and cut into bite-size pieces

Salt and freshly ground black pepper, to taste

1½ cups chicken broth

2 large tomatoes, peeled, seeded and coarsely chopped

1 medium onion, chopped

1 leek, white part only, cleaned and sliced

2 medium carrots, peeled and chopped

1 pear, peeled and diced

½ cup raisins or sliced dates

Cooked couscous, if desired

¼ cup toasted pine nuts

1. Combine cumin, cinnamon, ginger and coriander, and divide mixture in half.

2. In a large nonstick skillet, heat 1 Tbsp of the oil over high heat; add lamb, half the spice mixture and salt and pepper to taste. Brown the lamb well on all sides, then transfer it to the slow-cooker, draining any fat from the skillet.

3. Heat remaining oil and spice mixture in the same skillet over medium heat until aromatic, about 20 to 30 seconds. Add to slow-cooker. Add the chicken broth, tomatoes, onion, leek, carrots, pear and raisins; stir well.

4. Cover and cook on high 4 to 5 hours, or on low 8 to 10 hours, until lamb is tender.

5. To serve, spoon lamb mixture over couscous, if using, and sprinkle the pine nuts over all.

PER SERVING: **679 cal, 80 g pro, 25 g car, 4 g fiber, 28 g fat (8 g sat fat), 246 mg chol, 765 mg sod**

Lentil & Ham Stew

SLOW-COOKER • SERVES 6 • PREP: 12 MINUTES • COOK: 4 TO 5 HR ON HIGH,
7 TO 9 HR ON LOW

3 cups diced ham

2 cups dried lentils

2 cups *each* diced carrots and celery

1 cup chopped onion

1 Tbsp minced garlic

4 cups water

1 tsp dried oregano

2 cans (10½ oz each) condensed chicken broth

¼ tsp *each* salt and pepper

1 bag (6 oz) baby spinach leaves

2 Tbsp fresh lemon juice

GARNISH: lemon slices

1. Mix all ingredients except spinach leaves and lemon juice in a 3½-qt or larger slow-cooker. Cover and cook on high 4 to 5 hours or on low 7 to 9 hours until lentils are tender.

2. Stir in spinach leaves, cover and cook 5 minutes or until tender. Stir in lemon juice.

PER SERVING: **426 cal, 37 g pro, 51 g car, 11 g fiber, 9 g fat (3 g sat), 41 mg chol, 1,758 mg sod**

TIP Don't be tempted to add more liquid than called for. Foods give up quite a bit as they cook and any extra dilutes the flavor.

Braised Pork & Apple Stew

ONE POT • SERVES 4 • PREP: 8 MINUTES • TOTAL TIME: 30 MINUTES

2 tsp vegetable oil

1 pork tenderloin (about 1 lb), cut into 1½-in. chunks

¼ tsp *each* salt and freshly ground black pepper

1 Tbsp all-purpose flour

1 can (14½ oz) chicken broth

2 Gala apples, cored and each cut into 8 wedges

8 very small red potatoes, halved

1 cup baby carrots

½ tsp dried thyme

3 Tbsp honey-Dijon mustard

1. Heat oil in 5- to 6-qt pot over medium-high heat. While oil heats, sprinkle pork with salt and pepper, and coat with flour. Cook pork 4 minutes until browned, turning once; remove to a plate.

2. Add broth, apples, potatoes, carrots and thyme to pot and bring to a boil. Cover, reduce heat and simmer 12 minutes, or until potatoes are tender. Stir in pork and mustard. Cover and simmer 4 to 5 minutes, until pork is just cooked through.

PER SERVING: 364 cal, 29 g pro, 47 g car, 5 g fiber, 7 g fat (2 g sat fat), 74 mg chol, 555 mg sod

Pork & Cider Stew

SLOW-COOKER • SERVES 5 • PREP: 15 MINUTES • COOK: 7 TO 9 HR ON LOW

2 medium sweet potatoes (1¼ lb), peeled and cut in ¾-in. pieces

3 small parsnips or carrots, peeled and cut in ½-in.-thick slices

1 cup chopped onion

2-lb boneless pork shoulder, cut in 1-in. pieces

1 large Granny Smith apple, peeled, cored and coarsely chopped

¼ cup all-purpose flour

¾ tsp salt

½ tsp *each* dried sage and thyme

¼ tsp pepper

1 cup apple cider

1. Layer sweet potatoes, parsnips, onion, pork and apple in a 3½-qt or larger slow-cooker.

2. Stir flour, salt, sage, thyme and pepper in a small bowl to mix. Add cider; stir until smooth. Pour over meat and vegetables.

3. Cover and cook on low 7 to 9 hours until pork and sweet potatoes are tender when pierced.

PER SERVING: **631 cal, 34 g pro, 47 g car, 6 g fiber, 33 g fat (11 g sat fat), 129 mg chol, 485 mg sod**

Pork-Tomato Stew

ONE POT • SERVES 4 • PREP: 10 MINUTES • TOTAL TIME: 1 HR

1 lb well-trimmed boneless pork shoulder (Boston Butt), cut in ¾-in. chunks

3 medium red potatoes

1 large yellow summer squash or zucchini

1 can (14½ oz) diced tomatoes with roasted garlic

1 can (14½ oz) chicken broth

1 tsp *each* ground cumin and dried oregano

½ tsp *each* salt and pepper

1 can (about 15 oz) chickpeas, rinsed

1. Coat a 4- to 6-qt saucepan with nonstick spray. Add pork; sauté 5 minutes or until browned.

2. Meanwhile cut potatoes in 1-in. chunks (2⅓ cups), and dice squash (2 cups). Add to pork along with remaining ingredients except chickpeas.

3. Bring to a boil, reduce heat, cover and simmer, stirring a few times, 40 to 45 minutes until pork is tender. Stir in chickpeas and heat through.

PER SERVING: 383 cal, 30 g pro, 38 g car, 6 g fiber, 12 g fat (3 g sat fat), 76 mg chol, 1,402 mg sod

Quick Tex-Mex Pork Stew

ONE POT • SERVES 4 • PREP: 40 MINUTES • TOTAL TIME: 1 HR 20 MINUTES

1 Tbsp oil

¾ lb well-trimmed boneless pork shoulder (Boston Butt), cut in ¾-in. chunks

3 cups coarsely chopped onions

2 Tbsp minced garlic

4 cups chicken broth

2 ancho chiles, stems and seeds removed, chiles rinsed

1 tsp dried oregano

1 can (15 to 16 oz) white hominy or corn kernels, drained

TOPPINGS: shredded lettuce, chopped plum tomatoes and slivered onion

1. Heat oil in 3-qt saucepan over medium-high heat. Add pork and brown on all sides, 3 to 5 minutes. Add onions and garlic, and cook, stirring occasionally, 5 minutes or until lightly browned.

2. Add broth, chiles and oregano. Bring to a simmer, cover and cook 1 hour or until pork is tender. Add hominy and simmer, uncovered, 10 minutes.

3. Skim off and discard any skins from the chiles. Ladle stew into soup bowls and serve with toppings.

PER SERVING: 353 cal, 23 g pro,
34 g car, 7 g fiber, 14 g fat (3 g sat fat),
58 mg chol, 1,230 mg sod

Mexican Pork & Sweet Potato Stew

ONE POT • SERVES 6 • PREP: 10 MINUTES • TOTAL TIME: 30 MINUTES

1 Tbsp olive oil

1¼ lb pork tenderloin, cut bite-size

1½ lb sweet potatoes, peeled and cubed

2 poblano chile peppers, seeded and sliced

1 cup chopped onion

1 Tbsp chopped garlic

½ tsp ground cumin

¼ tsp ground cinnamon

1 can (14 oz) reduced-sodium chicken broth

½ cup water

1 cup frozen corn kernels

1½ cups salsa

Garnish: chopped cilantro, tortilla strips

1. Heat 2 tsp of the oil in a deep nonstick skillet. Add pork; cook over medium-high heat 7 minutes or until browned. Transfer pork to a plate.

2. Heat remaining 1 tsp oil in skillet. Add potatoes, peppers and onion. Cover; cook 5 minutes, stirring, until peppers and onion soften slightly.

3. Stir in garlic, cumin and cinnamon; cook a few seconds until fragrant. Add broth and water; bring to a boil. Add corn; cover and cook 5 minutes or until vegetables soften.

4. Stir in salsa and pork; heat through. Sprinkle servings with cilantro and tortilla strips if desired.

PER SERVING: **268 cal, 23 g pro, 31 g car, 4 g fiber, 5 g fat (1 g sat fat), 61 mg chol, 474 mg sod**

Pork Goulash

SLOW-COOKER • SERVES 6 • PREP: 5 MINUTES • COOK: 7 TO 9 HR ON LOW

1¼-lb boneless pork butt
(shoulder), cut in 1-in. chunks

1 can (14 oz) crushed tomatoes
in purée

1 packet beefy-onion soup mix
(from a 2.2-oz box)

2 Tbsp sweet paprika

2 tsp minced garlic

1 tsp caraway seeds

¾ cup reduced-fat sour cream

3 Tbsp snipped fresh dill

1. Mix all ingredients except sour cream and dill in a 3-qt or larger slow-cooker.

2. Cover and cook on low 7 to 9 hours until pork is tender. Stir in sour cream and dill.

PER SERVING: **300 cal, 20 g pro, 11 g car, 1 g fiber, 20 g fat (7 g sat fat), 77 mg chol, 614 mg sod**

Ham & Mushroom Strata

OVEN • SERVES 8 • PREP: 50 MINUTES • TOTAL TIME: 1 HR 50 MINUTES

1 Tbsp stick butter

1 cup finely chopped onion

10 oz mushrooms, sliced

1 piece (8 oz) boneless smoked ham, cubed

1 bag (16 oz) broccoli florets, steamed

8 slices sandwich bread, cubed

6 oz fontina cheese, shredded (1½ cups)

6 large eggs

3 cups whole milk

¼ tsp pepper

1. You'll need a shallow 3-qt baking dish lightly coated with nonstick spray.

2. Melt butter in a large skillet. Add onion; sauté until tender. Add mushrooms; sauté until browned and dry. Stir in ham and broccoli.

3. Spread half the bread cubes in prepared baking dish. Top with ham mixture and half the cheese. Scatter remaining bread over top. Whisk eggs, milk and pepper in a large bowl until blended. Pour evenly over bread; sprinkle with remaining cheese. Bake and serve, or cover and refrigerate up to 1 day.

4. To SERVE: Heat oven to 350°F. Bake uncovered 1 hour or until top is puffed and lightly browned, and a wooden pick inserted in center comes out dry.

PER SERVING: **365 cal, 26 g pro, 24 g car, 3 g fiber, 19 g fat (9 g sat fat), 221 mg chol, 1,217 mg sod**

Sausage-Stuffed Squash

SKILLET • SERVES 4 • PREP: 10 MINUTES • TOTAL TIME: 21 MINUTES

4 medium summer squash (zucchini, yellow or a combination), halved lengthwise

12 oz Italian pork sausages, casing removed

1 can (14.5 oz) diced tomatoes in juice with roasted pepper, not drained

1. Scoop flesh from squash, leaving a ¼-in.-thick shell. Dice flesh.

2. Cook sausage and diced squash in a large nonstick skillet, breaking up sausage with a spoon, 5 minutes or until browned and cooked. Remove to a bowl; stir in tomatoes.

3. Put squash halves cut side down in skillet. Add 2 Tbsp water, cover and cook 2 minutes. Turn squash over, cover and cook 2 minutes until crisp-tender. Fill with sausage mixture. Cover; cook over low heat 2 minutes to reheat.

PER SERVING: 383 cal, 15 g pro, 19 g car, 3 g fiber, 27 g fat (10 g sat fat), 65 mg chol, 1,091 mg sod

Cumin Roast Pork with Dried Fruit

OVEN • SERVES 8 • PREP: 15 MINUTES • TOTAL TIME: 1 HR 15 MINUTES

1 pkg (6 oz) mixed dried fruit, coarsely chopped (1 cup)

2½ lb boneless pork loin

1½ tsp ground cumin

½ tsp salt

¼ tsp pepper

1. Heat oven to 375°F. Soak fruit in 1 cup boiling water 15 minutes. You'll need a small roasting pan and kitchen string.

2. Make a long cut down center of pork, not all the way through. Open like a book. Mix cumin, salt and pepper; sprinkle ½ tsp of mixture over cut surface.

3. Drain fruit; save liquid. Arrange fruit over one side of pork. Fold over other side to enclose filling. Tie in several places with kitchen string. Rub meat with rest of cumin mixture. Place in pan.

4. Roast 50 minutes, or until a meat thermometer inserted in center registers 160°F. Remove to cutting board; let rest 10 minutes.

5. Meanwhile, add fruit liquid to pan and stir over high heat to dissolve browned bits on bottom. Simmer 4 minutes to reduce slightly. Serve with pork.

PER SERVING: **316 cal, 30 g pro, 13 g car, 2 g fiber, 16 g fat (6 g sat fat), 88 mg chol, 206 mg sod**

Pork Pozole

SLOW-COOKER • SERVES 6 • PREP: 10 MINUTES • COOK: 7 TO 9 HR ON LOW

2-lb boneless pork butt, fat trimmed, cut in bite-size chunks

1 jar (12 oz) recaito (see Note)

1 can (15 to 16 oz) hominy, rinsed

GARNISH: chopped cilantro and radishes

1. Put pork and recaito in a 3-qt or larger slow-cooker. Stir to mix and coat.

2. Cover and cook on low 7 to 9 hours, until pork is very tender.

3. Stir in hominy, cover and cook 10 minutes to heat hominy. Top with garnish if desired.

PER SERVING: 287 cal, 30 g pro, 10 g car, 2 g fiber, 13 g fat (4 g sat fat), 103 mg chol, 657 mg sod

TIP Good with warm flour tortillas.

NOTE Recaito is a thicker-than-salsa, cilantro-based seasoning that's used to add flavor to rice, beans, soups and stews.

White Bean & Sausage Soup

SLOW-COOKER • SERVES 5 • PREP: 6 MINUTES • COOK: 7 TO 9 HR ON LOW

1 pkg (1.8 oz) leek soup and recipe mix

1 lb reduced-fat kielbasa or Italian sausages

2 cans (16 oz each) white kidney beans (cannellini), rinsed

6 oz Swiss chard, coarsely chopped

SERVE WITH: grated Parmesan cheese

1. Mix soup mix with 6 cups water in a 3½-qt or larger slow-cooker. Add kielbasa and beans.

2. Cover and cook on low 7 to 9 hours. Remove kielbasa with tongs to cutting board; cut into diagonal slices.

3. Stir kielbasa slices and Swiss chard into slow-cooker. Cover and cook 10 minutes just until chard is wilted. Serve with grated Parmesan, if desired.

PER SERVING: 364 cal, 23 g pro, 32 g car, 8 g fiber, 15 g fat (5 g sat fat), 57 mg chol, 1,661 mg sod

White Bean & Sausage Cassoulet

SKILLET & OVEN • SERVES 8 • PREP: 20 MINUTES • COOK: 30 MINUTES

2 tsp oil

3 links (10 oz) Italian sausage

2 medium carrots, thinly sliced

2 stalks celery, sliced

1 large onion, chopped

2 tsp minced garlic

3 cans (15.5 oz each) Great Northern beans, rinsed

2 cans (14.5 oz each) fire-roasted diced tomatoes

½ cup water

1 tsp dried thyme leaves

SEASONED CRUMB TOPPING

2 tsp oil

1 tsp minced garlic

2 cups coarse fresh bread crumbs from a baguette

2 Tbsp *each* grated Parmesan and chopped parsley

1. Heat oven to 375°F. You'll need a rimmed baking sheet lined with foil.

2. Heat oil in a 5-qt pot over medium heat. Brown sausages on all sides until cooked through, about 6 minutes. Remove to plate.

3. In fat remaining in saucepan, sauté carrots, celery, onion and garlic until golden, about 5 minutes.

4. Cut sausages into ¼-in.-thick slices. Add sausages, beans, tomatoes and their juices, water and thyme to saucepan. Simmer, covered, 30 minutes or until heated through and flavors are blended.

5. TOPPING: Toss oil and garlic with bread crumbs; spread on prepared baking sheet. Bake 15 to 20 minutes, tossing once, until toasted. Cool slightly; stir in Parmesan and parsley. Serve over cassoulet.

PER SERVING: **316 cal, 16 g pro, 37 g car, 10 g fiber, 14 g fat (4 g sat fat), 28 mg chol, 979 mg sod**

Sausage & Peppers Meat Loaf

SLOW-COOKER • SERVES 8 • PREP: 10 MINUTES • COOK: 5 TO 8 HR ON LOW

1½ cups Barilla Sweet Peppers & Garlic pasta sauce

1 lb hot or sweet Italian pork sausage, removed from casings

1 lb lean ground beef

¾ cup *each* fresh bread crumbs and finely chopped onion

¼ cup shredded Romano or Parmesan cheese

1 large egg

2 tsp minced garlic

2 tsp fennel seeds (optional)

½ tsp *each* salt and pepper

1. To ease removal of loaf from cooker, fold two 24-in.-long pieces foil in half lengthwise twice. Place strips across each other, forming a "+" in bottom of a 3½-qt or larger slow-cooker. Press strips against inside of cooker, letting ends hang over outside.

2. Mix ½ cup pasta sauce with remaining ingredients in a large bowl until well blended. Form into a 7½ x 4½ x 2½-in. loaf. Place in cooker.

3. Cover and cook on low 5 to 8 hours until a meat thermometer inserted in the center of the loaf registers 165°F.

4. Heat rest of sauce; serve with meat loaf.

PER SERVING: 410 cal, 21 g pro, 8 g car, 1 g fiber, 32 g fat (12 g sat fat), 115 mg chol, 893 mg sod

TIP Try a pasta salad on the side. Leftover meat loaf makes great sandwiches.

Italian Veal Stew

SLOW-COOKER • SERVES 6 • PREP: 10 MINUTES • COOK: 7 TO 9 HR ON LOW

¾ cup *each* chicken broth and dry white wine

¼ cup all-purpose flour

1½ lb veal shoulder, cut for stew

1½ cups diced carrots

¾ cup diced celery

¼ cup chopped shallots

1 bay leaf

2 tsp chopped fresh rosemary

1 can (14½ oz) diced tomatoes, drained

3 cups cooked orzo

GARNISH: grated lemon zest, chopped parsley

1. Whisk broth, wine and flour in a 3½-qt or larger slow-cooker until blended. Stir in remaining ingredients except orzo.

2. Cover; cook on low 7 to 9 hours until veal is very tender. Sprinkle with lemon zest and parsley. Serve with orzo.

PER SERVING: 332 cal, 30 g pro, 43 g car, 4 g fiber, 4 g fat (1 g sat fat), 95 mg chol, 251 mg sod

Dilled Veal & Vegetable Stew

SLOW-COOKER • SERVES 6 • PREP: 10 MINUTES • COOK: 7 TO 9 HR ON LOW
FINISH: 15 MINUTES ON HIGH

1¾-lb veal shoulder, cut up for stew

1 can (14½ oz) whole tomatoes in juice, coarsely chopped, undrained

12 small boiling onions, peeled, cut in half

8 oz baby carrots

¼ cup dry white wine (optional)

½ tsp *each* pepper and minced garlic

1 can (10¾ oz) condensed cream of mushroom soup

8 oz sliced mushrooms

¼ cup chopped fresh dill

1. Mix all ingredients except the mushroom soup, mushrooms and dill in a 4-qt or larger slow-cooker.

2. Cover and cook on low 7 to 9 hours until veal and vegetables are tender.

3. Stir in soup until blended. Add mushrooms; cover and cook on high 15 minutes, or until mushrooms are tender. Stir in dill.

PER SERVING: **271 cal, 28 g pro, 14 g car, 2 g fiber, 11 g fat (4 g sat fat), 116 mg chol, 661 mg sod**

TIP Serve over egg noodles.

Osso Buco

4 lb veal shanks

½ cup flour

Salt and freshly ground black pepper, to taste

5 Tbsp olive oil

¼ cup butter

2 yellow onions, finely chopped

2 carrots, peeled and finely chopped

1½ cups dry white wine or dry white vermouth

1½ cups chicken broth

1 can (14½ oz) plum tomatoes, drained and chopped

GREMOLATA

Zest of 2 lemons

4 cloves garlic, smashed with the flat edge of a knife

⅓ cup chopped parsley

PER SERVING: 431 cal, 46 g pro, 19 g car, 3 g fiber, 18 g fat (7 g sat fat), 197 mg chol, 630 mg sod

1. Pat veal shanks dry with paper towel. Mix flour with salt and pepper on a plate. Evenly coat shanks in mixture, shaking off excess.

2. Heat 2 Tbsp each of the oil and butter in a large skillet over medium-high heat. When very hot, add half the veal shanks and brown them well on all sides. Repeat with 2 more Tbsp of the oil, the remaining butter and veal. Place browned shanks in a 4-qt or larger slow-cooker.

3. Discard fat in skillet. Add remaining oil; heat over medium heat. Add onions and carrots; cook, stirring, until onion is softened, about 5 minutes. Add wine and broth; bring to a boil. Add tomatoes; cook, stirring, until sauce is reduced to desired consistency, then pour over shanks. Sauce should come about halfway up shanks.

4. Cover and cook on low 7 to 8 hours, until veal is fork-tender and falling off the bone.

5. Transfer the Osso Buco to a serving platter and keep warm. Skim any excess fat from the cooking liquid. For a smoother-textured sauce, purée with an immersion blender or food mill.

6. GREMOLATA: Combine ingredients in a small food processor. Pulse until mixture is finely chopped.

7. Spoon the sauce over veal shanks and sprinkle gremolata over top. Serve hot, with small spoons for scooping out the delicious bone marrow.

Photo Credits

First published in 2009 in the United States of America by Filipacchi Publishing
1633 Broadway
New York, NY 10019

Design: Patricia Fabricant
Editing: Lauren Kuczala
Production: Lynn Scaglione

ISBN 13: 978-1-933231-62-4

Library of Congress
Control Number: 2009923652

Printed in China

Page 2: Joey de Leo; page 6: Jacqueline Hopkins; page 8: Charles Schiller; page 9: Mary Ellen Bartley; page 11: John Uher; page 12: Anastassios Mentis; page 14: John Uher; page 16: Dasha Wright; page 17: Mark Thomas; page 19: Frances Janisch; pages 20, 21: Dasha Wright; page 22: Charles Schiller; page 23: James Baigrie; page 25: Joey de Leo; page 27: Mary Ellen Bartley; page 28: Dasha Wright; page 30: John Uher; page 31: Jacqueline Hopkins; page 32: John Uher; page 35: Jim Franco; page 36: Charles Schiller; page 37: John Uher; page 38: Mary Ellen Bartley; page 41: Ellie Miller; page 42: Mark Ferri; page 44: Kate Sears; page 45: Charles Schiller; page 47: Mary Ellen Bartley; page 48: Frances Janisch; page 51: Courtesy U.S. Apple Association; page 52: Anastassios Mentis; page 54: Jim Franco; page 57: Kate Sears; page 59: Mary Ellen Bartley; page 60: Charles Schiller; page 63: Mary Ellen Bartley; page 64: John Uher; page 65: Dasha Wright; page 67: Courtesy Australian Lamb; page 68: John Uher; page 71: Anastassios Mentis; page 72: Dasha Wright; page 74: John Uher; page 75: Charles Schiller; page 76: Mary Ellen Bartley; page 78: Charles Schiller; page 79: Mark Thomas; pages 81, 82, 85: John Uher; page 86: Mary Ellen Bartley; page 89: Ellie Miller; page 90: Frances Janisch; page 91: Kate Sears; page 92: John Uher, page 95: Joey de Leo.